STARTED IN THE DM

**Dawn Dickson-Akpoghene &
Frederick Akpoghene**

Illustrated By: Sampson The Artist

Autliers LLC
Miami, FL

Copyright © 2021 by Dawn Dickson-Akpoghene & Frederick Akpoghene

All rights reserved.

Started in the DM: Using Social Media to Find the One

Author website: startedinthedm.com
Email: startedinthedm@gmail.com
Connect: @startedinthedm

Illustrations by: Sampson the Artist
Email: sampsontheartist@gmail.com
Connect: @sammiedoesit

ISBN-13: 978-0-578-98716-3
Published in the United States by Autliers, LLC, Miami, Florida.

Photography by: Jehan, LLC (2020)
Edited by: Few Editorial & Creative Suite

Table of Contents

♥ ♥ ♥ ♥

Preface		5
Introduction		8
Chapter 1	Getting Started	16
Chapter 2	Sliding in The DMs	26
Chapter 3	Turn-Ons & Turn-Offs	37
Chapter 4	Moving Offline	46
Chapter 5	How to Have A Great Date	54
Chapter 6	Moving Up the Ladder	67

Preface

Written by: Dawn Dickson-Akpoghene

We've all been there: single, scrolling through social media, pausing on someone attractive, and thinking about reaching out but never do to avoid looking thirsty. I get it! Most want to meet someone and have a dating life but don't know where to start.

I used to create profiles on dating sites and apps and then delete them after a week or so because it quickly became overwhelming.

Between dealing with the men who would Google me and ask for business advice and those who wanted to "chat" online for hours or *WYD* me to death without asking me on a real date—I didn't have time to manage it all. The number of conversations I had to weed through to finally see what was truly there in this huge option pool was ridiculous. In addition, I honestly didn't want certain people to see me on those dating sites (i.e., friends, peers, customers, investors, family).

One of the greatest challenges was figuring out how I only interact with people that I wanted to interact with in this way and somehow curate who knows I am single. I gave up on dating sites forever. I tried to meet people "the old fashioned" way (in person) but soon realized that, using this route, it would be difficult to ever meet men outside of my work and immediate friends' networks. What I knew for sure was that I didn't want to date any of them already in my close-knit circle.

I decided to take time off from dating altogether and work on myself. During this time, I deleted all of my dating app profiles, and I removed Instagram from my phone for four months. While away from the social media world, a close friend of mine told me a sweet story of how she'd met her current bae on Instagram.

"He slid in my DMs," she said. "I gave him a chance, and it was 'happily ever after' from then on!" I could only relate to the men "sliding in the DMs" part of the story.

Men were constantly in my DMs being friendly, but I never gave them a chance. Her experience made me rethink my attitude toward men in my DMs, and I decided to be more open-minded.

I reinstalled Instagram on my phone with a fresh perspective, and within 7 days, I got the DM that changed my life…

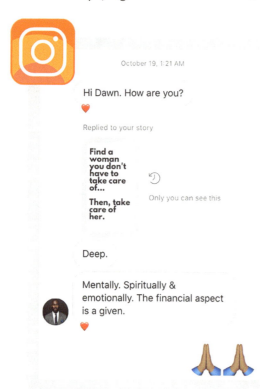

He had been in my DMs for a while—casually, like many others, but I never gave the messages much attention.

This time around, however, my fresh perspective allowed me to put my guard down and engage in a conversation with him, which is something I would've never done otherwise.

Now, after building a successful relationship together, we decided to write this book to share our experiences from both a male and female perspective on dating online, using apps, and ultimately finding "the one" in the DMs.

For lack of better words: We started in the DMs, and now we are here…

I hope you find inspiration in our story and use the tips we share to find the person of your dreams. It is possible!

Intro-duction

With over 40 million Americans active on dating websites, the possibility of finding love online has never been this high or this overwhelming. Your 'bae' is probably online right now, and all you need to do is find a way to connect. Sure, it sounds simple, but it would be a lie to say that online dating is easy. It's not.

Online dating can be very awkward, cumbersome, dangerous, and time-consuming. There are so many mistakes you can make when venturing into this lane for the first time. Even those who are experienced with online dating can still struggle with it. And it's not rare for a professional to go on several dates before finding the right person.

If you have the time and energy, you can easily succeed in the dating game by going on as many dates as possible, and sooner or later, finding that person that clicks with you. But, if you're a busy executive, high-profile influencer, or entrepreneur, finding the time and energy for so many dates is difficult. This is why we decided to write a book from the perspective of the "busy entrepreneur". It represents our lifestyles and our dating journey.

This book is written to help those who are not exactly comfortable putting themselves out there to find love for many reasons. It may be because of your schedule, personal brand, professional image, or need to navigate things that the average person doesn't have to deal with—like public reputation.

While there's plenty of advice out there on these topics, the strategies you'll learn here are tailored *for entrepreneurs.*

This is a guide designed to assist you with your online dating journey, from beginning to happy ending. You'll learn ultra-specific tips and time-saving strategies for online dating that include how to:
- Create an attractive profile
- Find someone that aligns with you
- Catch his or her attention
- Engage them in conversation
- Go out on a date in "real life"
- Build a relationship
- and more!

In the following chapters, we will dissect the online dating process and teach you how you can succeed in finding love online without sacrificing too much time and attention.

Let's get started.

Online Dating for Entrepreneurs

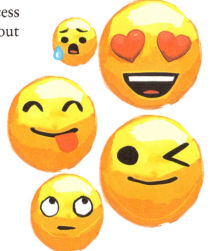

Anyone that has ventured into entrepreneurship would agree that entrepreneurs are a unique blend of creatives, risk-takers, and innovators who are not afraid to invest time, money, and resources into things they believe in. You would also agree that entrepreneurs don't have the schedule flexibility of most people working 9-5.

Entrepreneurs generally struggle with the following:

- Work-life balance

STARTED IN THE DM

- Maintaining a self-care practice
- Turning business 'off' and personal 'on' in social settings (digital and in-person)

Work-Life Balance

If there's one thing most successful entrepreneurs have in common, it's their focus on time management. Running a business successfully requires plenty of time, dedication, and attention. And although we all have the same 24 hours in a day, as an entrepreneur that time has to be maximized. Time is one currency that we can never get back. Many entrepreneurs suffer from poor work-life balance because it is very easy to get caught up in work and neglect personal needs. Sleep, a balanced diet, and our dating lives are often left on the back burner. As mentioned before, the typical way most master online dating is by spending hours each day engaging with the platforms and going on as many dates as possible.

The problem with this strategy is that it's not practical for an entrepreneur. You need a lot of time dedicated to your business, which means the time you have for dating is limited. Simple things like determining which dating platform to direct your energy can be overwhelming and discouraging. We don't want you to have to dive into online dating on your own seeing little success and eventually quitting. We want to save you time, so you don't end up wasting months in this process.

Self-Care

The number one mistake that entrepreneurs make is allowing their busy work schedules to take priority over their self-care practices. They are often on their phones or laptops working all hours of the day. We even sleep with our phones near our beds, and it's usually the first thing we check when we wake up. These practices can be offensive to potential partners. This lack of self-care and the inability to be fully present during some moments are habits that push people away.

10

INTRODUCTION

A major challenge that successful people face in online dating is determining the best representation of themselves to post online and also learning how to turn small talk into engaging, meaningful conversations.

That said, the good news is that these habits can be easily corrected and replaced with healthier, more balanced practices for self-care that will result in immediate changes in your life. When you are balanced within yourself, you can be a better boss, leader, partner, friend, and parent. You are overall a better person when your needs are met.

Meeting your needs starts with you, not another person. If you don't take care of yourself and make yourself a priority first, no one else can. So, the first step in finding love is giving the love to yourself that you desire from others. The energy of self-love radiates from you, and it's attractive to everyone that comes in contact with you.

Connecting on a Personal Level

Yes, we know you are a boss, and you are smart, intelligent, and accomplished. But what else, besides your business acumen and financial status, makes you, you? That is what a prospective partner wants to hear about, not your resume and bio. Many do not want to be vulnerable and show their other side but turning the brand off and putting your guard down will get the best results.

Day One Mistakes

In trying to find love online, there's a tendency to make several easily avoidable mistakes from day one. **Here are nine common ones to avoid:**

STARTED IN THE DM

Not picking the right platforms

There are a number of online dating platforms and each has a different vibe. Take time to research their benefits and candidate pools to make sure they align with your goals.

Poor dating profile optimization

Select profile photos that show your range, not just one side of you. Mix it up and show them who you are. Don't say too much in the bio—just say enough to spark interest and conversation.

Not knowing how to break the ice

Starting a conversation with hey and a general compliment does not open the door for a conversation. Why? Because it typically ends with a one-word response and a dead end. Break the ice with open-ended questions.

Putting too much stock on online chatting

There is only so much you can text about, and tone can't be interpreted over text. You must do things the old-fashioned way and get on the phone. Facetime would be even better to make sure you aren't being catfished. (Yes, this still happens all the time.)

Struggling with the transition to real-life dating

How long are you going to text and talk before you meet up? Don't hesitate to start thinking about great ways to transition into real-life dating.

Not picking the right dates

The point of a date is to get to know each other better, catch a vibe, and see if your interests align. Movie theaters and loud venues are not the places for that.

INTRODUCTION

Not knowing how to behave on a real-life date

This is not a networking event. You are not at an interview. You are not on stage. Take off the mask!

Not doing enough research

Is the person you're dating who they say they are? Fact-check before wasting your time.

Not knowing when to quit

Are you not feeling the vibe? Don't ignore the signs. Move on.

Chapter 1
Getting Started the Right Way

STARTED IN THE DM

THE MAIN OBJECTIVE OF ONLINE DATING IS TO MEET SOMEONE YOU WILL BE COMPATIBLE WITH IN REAL LIFE.

This is an important point most online dating newbies overlook. They get caught up in an online persona and think that it's a full and true representation of that person in real life, which is usually not the case.

While it's easy to get drawn into the fatal habit of swiping right, finding a match, and chatting up as many people that you're attracted to—it's vital to remember that there's a process to succeeding at

16

online dating.

To maximize your chances of finding love, don't be so quick to chat with everyone you find attractive. There are certain steps you should follow even before you slide into the DMs of your crushes and potential dates.

Here are what we call the three steps of getting started:

Step 1— Decide What You Are Looking For

A common mistake made by both male and female entrepreneurs who want to date is not knowing exactly what they are looking for. If they have zero ideas about the types of people they want to meet, where those people hang out, or how to make themselves available to potential matches, it's failure waiting to happen.

Dating apps can be very superficial because they are based on looks and captions. There is no real way to feel the vibe or personality of someone online. You simply meet their "representative", and even then, there are key things you must identify to determine if they are aligned with you. If you've been swiping right and instantly texting the profiles of everyone who looks good to you, then you have been using the wrong strategy. Not having "a type" wastes everyone's time. What do we mean by type?

To figure out what you want, you have to ask yourself some serious questions and be honest with yourself:

- What are the qualities I liked the most in my previous partners?
- What behaviors are deal breakers in a partner?
- What turns me on when I meet or interact with someone?
- What do I like doing and talking about?

STARTED IN THE DM

- What type of lifestyle do I prefer?
- What is my communication preference?
- What are my expectations around communication and time spent?
- Do I have a preference regarding children?
- Do I have a preference regarding geographic location?
- Do we have to share the same religious/spiritual beliefs?
- What are my love languages?
- Do I want a serious relationship, or am I in it for fun?

These are vulnerable questions, but it's exactly where you should start. You can go further with this by taking various dating personality and online matchmaking tests that can help in identifying potential partners. Some popular tests include MBTI, DiSC, PATH, and BEIT.

Knowing what you want is essential, as it helps to minimize the time spent with incompatible people.

Before you send a DM or swipe right, it's best to take time to review the profile of your interest and do a little investigation. Go through their pictures and read their captions. Ask yourself, "Are the things they say aligned with the type of person I want to be associated with?" Doing this helps because many people have profile images that don't accurately represent their true personalities.

Read the headlines, bios, captions, interests, and about sections of every profile of interest to see if they match your interests. However, you shouldn't take this as an excuse to go too far and rule everyone out before you have the chance to talk to them. It's only a screening measure to weed out the immediate red flags.

CHAPTER 1 - GETTING STARTED THE RIGHT WAY

That said, you should also pay attention to your choice of dating platform. Getting this right early will save you a lot of headache and heartache in the long run. Finding the right platform can take some time and research, but it will be time well spent.

Don't be afraid to use paid dating sites that offer more specific search capabilities than popular, free dating platforms. If you are looking for a particular type of person, you should be on the platforms where they are. The key is to do your research and find the dating websites that fit your requirements and are likely to be where your types frequently visit.

For example, Tinder is commonly known for "hook-ups"; of course, not everyone on the platform is there for just that. Others like Match. com, eHarmony, Hinge, Bumble, and The League promote finding love. Like many people, we had given up on dating sites and apps, so we ended up meeting on Instagram.

Although we were not looking for love on Instagram, we were open to it. Like most entrepreneurs, we use our Instagram accounts to post a mix of business and personal life. Social media sites make it easier to screen people than dating apps because they have a good amount of history to scroll through, which gives you a better sense of who people are and what they represent. Even though Instagram and Facebook are not considered "official" dating sites, countless couples have met on these platforms. This means the same rules apply!

Step 2 — Get Your Profile Right!

You have less than a second to impress your potential online match.

You read that right. You have less than one second. According to a study from Princeton, as humans, we decide if we are attracted to

STARTED IN THE DM

someone in less than a second of seeing them.
First impressions matter! Our point is that you can't afford to get your profile wrong because your potential match is judging you based on your profile. Luckily, creating an outstanding profile isn't that hard. There are three components you have to get right:

- Your profile photo
- Your bio/description
- Your supporting images that tell your story

The Profile Photo

Your profile photo is your first impression; unfortunately, most people use the wrong picture 99% of the time.

For females, using the sexiest and most seductive photo in your phone will end up sending the wrong message to guys. This is the reason many ladies have the wrong type of men sliding into their DMs. Sure, we agree that no one should be judged by their picture but by their personality.

However, as great as this sounds in theory, the facts show that you *will* be judged! Therefore, you need to decide how you want people to think of you.

Similarly, a common mistake that men make is using a display picture that isn't attractive to women or doesn't show them at their best. They don't give much thought

20

CHAPTER 1 - GETTING STARTED THE RIGHT WAY

to it. In a survey we conducted, most of the male respondents said that they don't give much thought to their profile picture and seldomly use the best picture they have.

Here are several tips for selecting your best profile picture:

- Since we all have blind spots for discovering our best pictures, ask your friends of the opposite sex to help you in selecting the pictures that best represent you.
- Try to upload a professional image taken in a comfortable environment, such as your home, a bar, or your place of work.
- Don't upload a photo that's blurry, has other people in it, or is difficult to see your face.
- Always upload recent pictures that accurately represent how you look today.
- Post a picture that has positive energy. A smile is always a great way to let others know you are fun to be with.
- Turn it into a conversation starter! Ask your online matches which pictures they liked the most, and then use the most voted photo as your profile picture.

The Bio

Writing about yourself is perhaps the most difficult aspect of creating an attractive profile. Keep your headline short, creative, and positive. The goal is to communicate what's unique about you and catch the attention of a potential match. For example, your profile can read, "Eddie Murphy movies, adventures, craft beer. If you like any of these three things, we'll get along great!"

- Don't write a lengthy story in your profile bio. It should be a few paragraphs (maximum of three paragraphs) talking about who you are, your unique interests and hobbies, and things that your potential match can most likely identify with.

- Treat your description like a CV and screen for any grammatical errors and misspellings. According to a survey by dating website EliteSingles, wrong spellings are one of the most despised traits of

STARTED IN THE DM

online dating.

- Don't be afraid to end with a call-to-action for your types. For example, you can end your description with, "Feel free to message me if you are an interesting person who is enthusiastic about traveling."

Step 3 — Isolate and Create Awareness

As you can see, things are moving fast, and you are almost ready to contact your crush. By now, you have a good idea of what you want, and your profile is well optimized to get it. To make things better, you have probably matched with someone you like, and you are thinking about reaching out to him or her. So, can you go ahead and do that now? Not so fast!

There is still a step to take before you slide into their DMs. You must create awareness.

This is letting them know you are alive, available, and interested (but not "thirsty"). Even though most people participating in online dating are ready to chat with strangers, you have to do your best to stand out. If you are not on an official dating site and only use social media (like Instagram, Facebook, or Twitter to connect with your crush), it could get even trickier.

There are various ways to go about putting yourself on someone's radar. Each platform offers different functionalities, so there's no "one approach fits all" solution in this case. However, it becomes easier once you remember that the idea is just to make them aware that you exist before they see you in their DMs.

Creating awareness creates a mutual interest. This way, when you eventually send a message, it will stand out, and they will be more likely to respond.

22

CHAPTER 1 - GETTING STARTED THE RIGHT WAY

> In our case, we exchanged a few casual messages over eight months before we engaged in a full conversation. He would comment on a story I posted, ask a question about something I shared, or ask me how my day was going. He never flirted or came on strong. These things made me comfortable with engaging with him online.

Dawn

> I can't remember how I started following her, but I know I was attracted to her physically, of course. Beyond what was physical, her business and spiritual-related content stood out to me as well. She had depth and was interesting. I wanted to get her attention but did not want to be like everyone else in her DMs. For that reason, I just commented on things she shared in her stories that resonated with me. I did that for several months before I attempted to have a conversation.

Frederick

Here are 3 recommendations for creating awareness across platforms:

1. Swipe Right

If you are on a dating platform that works with cross-matching, indicating interest by swiping right is the place to start. Even though many dating platforms allow you to send a message immediately without matching, try not to do that until you have swiped right.

2. Scroll Through Their Social Media

This step is a little time-consuming. In addition, it can sound a little creepy, but it's not. Once you have identified someone you like, take their name and do a quick Google search to find their other social media pages.

See if they have profiles on Facebook, Instagram, and other platforms that match their name and photos. This helps to confirm that they are who they say they are, and you can see the type of content they share. What people post says a lot about them.

3. Like & Comment

To create more awareness, you should scroll through their page and like a few pictures that catch your eye. Maybe even comment on a few photos, but by all means, please don't do too much! You want to come across as genuine and not as a creepy cyberstalker.

> When Dawn first checked out my profile, she went through and liked 50 posts!
> — **Frederick**

> OMG! It was more like 3! Stop exaggerating! Clearly my few "likes" made you feel special.
> — **Dawn**

CHAPTER 1 - GETTING STARTED THE RIGHT WAY

"Like" away, but don't be afraid to check out some of the comments on their posts as well to see the types of people they are engaging with. When you go through the posts of some attractive people online, it's not uncommon to see obnoxious comments from the opposite sex such as:

These comments are unflattery, and they are the last thing you want to do. To come across as genuine, you have to make concise, intelligent, and reasonable comments. Instead of telling a woman that she is beautiful and commenting on her curves, compliment her outfit, comment on the location or subject matter she is posting about. Contribute to the conversation. *That* will get her attention.

The reason you shouldn't jump on the flattery bandwagon is that as much as women like to be complimented about their beauty, they also want to be admired because of their depth and personality traits. Additionally, as you comment on the posts with her image, leave intelligent replies on other posts that don't contain her picture.

If she shares a lot of content around travel or yoga, drop relevant comments in response to those posts. Ladies, if your male crush is into cars or a certain brand, drop relevant comments, too.

You can even ask questions to get a response and show interest in what he or she is doing. Most people who are interested in meeting someone online don't take time to think about the right approach. Have a strategy! That'll be the reason you stand out. Once you get their attention and some engagement going, you are ready for the next step — the direct message to their inbox on the platform, aka the DMs.

Chapter 2
Sliding in the DM
♥ ♥ ♥ ♥

STARTED IN THE DM

BEFORE WRITING THIS CHAPTER, WE DID A SURVEY AND REALIZED THAT ONE OF THE TOP REASONS WHY PEOPLE GIVE UP ON ONLINE DATING IS BECAUSE THE PEOPLE THAT THEY ARE INTERESTED IN ARE NOT RESPONSIVE.

When sliding in someone's DMs, there is typically one of three possible outcomes:

- You fail to get any response at all.
- You get a response or two but are unable to spark a conversation.
- You get a response and maintain the engagement.

CHAPTER 2 - SLIDING IN THE DM

What separates scenario one from scenario three? The power of the first message. We discovered that in online dating, there is an art to sliding into the DMs, and what separates the winners from the losers is how they frame their first few messages.

To attract the attention of your love interest, you have to master the art of the conversation starter. Some people will advise you to be yourself and just say hello; meanwhile, others will tell you to craft an attention-grabbing story. While both approaches would work, the word choice is most often where people go wrong.

Crafting an Attention-Grabbing DM

If the person of interest is attractive or poppin' in any way, it is safe to assume that your crush most likely receives messages from multiple admirers every day. Therefore, to stand a chance, your initial message has to be unique and interesting enough to warrant a response.

Don't Go with "Hi" or Cheesy Pick-Up Lines

Most people who are new to online dating choose the easy way out by either saying "hi" or using a pick-up line. Don't do that.

While you can easily use "hi there" and "how are you doing" to break the ice in the physical world, you should know that a large part of our connection in real life is nonverbal.

According to a study conducted by Hinge, the "hey" and "hi there" are among the *top worst-performing DMs* on their platform.

29

STARTED IN THE DM

This is not surprising at all once you consider that online chatting is very different from real life. It's an unnatural way of communication, and the only thing your crush is seeing is your words in the text, not hearing your voice, feeling your energy, or observing your tone and mannerisms. That said, another thing you shouldn't do is turn to pick-up lines. Even though some of them can be good, most of them will make you come across as cheesy, awkward, and lame. The alternative is to use what we call thoughtful openers.

Be Thoughtful

There are no universal openers that work on everyone; however, by paying attention and following a few rules, you can start crafting messages that get more responses. Here's how:

1. Start with a Personal Question or Comment

Which of the following do you think will perform best?

A. *Hi! How are you doing?*

B. *What's up! How was your weekend?*

C. *I'm the kind that can't think of what to text to a beautiful girl, so here I am saying hi.*

D. *Hey, I saw in your profile that you liked traveling. Have you been to Fiji yet?*

If you guessed D, you picked the right answer. While the other options may work, you are more likely to get a response with option D, as long as your crush mentioned traveling in his or her description. What we found is that personal questions and comments make the best icebreakers because they demonstrate your attention to detail. Your crush feels special, and they appreciate that you took the time to learn more about them.

Many people will mention their interests and hobbies online in their

CHAPTER 2 - SLIDING IN THE DM

descriptions. All you have to do is make a comment or ask about these interests and hobbies, and you will stand out from the multitudes sending generic messages.

You can ask about a book, a movie or any activity referenced anywhere on their page. For instance:

- *Hey! I can see you like Afrobeats. I'm a big fan, too. Who is your favorite artist?*
- *Hello. As a big fan of cryptocurrencies, I noticed your profile says you are an expert. What coin do you trade the most?*
- *I can see you are a fan of X author. I love her books. Have you read any good books lately that you would recommend?*
- *How did you like the X movie? Is it worth seeing?*

The reason this works is that people like talking about themselves. Therefore, instead of only saying a general greeting or telling a story about yourself, this approach allows your crush to talk about themselves. This way, you increase your chances of getting replies and learn more about them.

Our first real conversation in the DMs really flowed well. He asked, "How has your journey been?" "Which one?" I replied. This opened the door for him to start a conversation and dig deeper into getting to know me.

Dawn

I previously tried to start a conversation with her by asking, "How is your day going?" But she responded with good and left it at that. She always responded, but she kept it short or just liked my comment. I knew I needed to try a different approach to get her talking.

Frederick

STARTED IN THE DM

2. Start with a Genuine Compliment

Another really good way to break the ice is with compliments, but don't take it to the extreme. Stay away from corny compliments like sexy, hot, or beautiful. Only use safe words like amazing, interesting, cool, etc., in describing your crush's personality and hobbies.

Also, don't make the mistake of solely fixating on your crush's profile photo. We discover that people respond more when you compliment their interests and hobbies.

For example:

- *Wow! I just read your blog, and you are such an amazing writer. I'm a writer too.*
- *I can see you've been on an exercising streak of 10 months. Great job! I wish I had your perseverance.*
- *I like how you advocate for blood donations. The world needs more people like you!*
- *Your photography skill is out of this world. What's your secret?*

3. Break the Ice with Charming Questions

Another way to break the ice is with questions your crush doesn't get often. The key here is to come across as a person who is really into them but doesn't know what to say. Here are some examples:

- *I'm a little confused. I came across your profile, and I don't know what to say to get your attention. Can you help me?*
- *What's that one thing that makes you special that's not on your profile?*
- *A dime for your thoughts—what are you thinking about right now? In other words, this is me not knowing what to say to get your*

attention!

- Okay, I know you probably have a thousand people texting you every day, but I just came across your profile and thought you were an interesting individual. I had no option but to say hi.

> **Those approaches would not work for me because I like a confident man. He broke the ice by telling me that he believes a man should be supportive of a woman in all ways. That was attractive.**
>
> **Dawn**

> **Some women like the shy guy approach, but I am an alpha male. So, that's not my style. However, when I was single, I would have been flattered if a woman approached me with those lines. I would respond.**
>
> **Frederick**

The Do's & Don'ts of Messaging

Now that you have broken the ice and got their attention, things are only getting started. Now you have to maintain the communication and build a connection that translates offline.

It is exciting to get the attention of someone you are interested in, and while that's great, staying in touch is the ultimate goal. You don't want to overwhelm him/her with communication after the first conversation. It is important to be mindful of how often you chat and what you chat about so that your crush doesn't lose interest and stop replying. Remember, they have a whole life, and more than likely, they are dating other people already.

Many people are unaware of these do's and don'ts to maintain a stable conversation with an online match.

Fortunately, keeping your crush's attention is not as complicated as it sounds. Some simple rules can drastically increase your chances.

The Don'ts

Don't Be a Fan: It's okay to be attracted to someone, respect their accomplishments, and admire their work—but no one wants to be idolized. People don't want to date a fan. They want to date a friend. Even if you are in awe of them, keep it cool.

Don't Conduct an Interview: One major complaint we hear from women is feeling like they are being interviewed by men. Guys, please stop this! And while there's nothing wrong with keeping the conversation alive, don't fire off questions just because. Volunteer your own answers to those questions sometimes and share things about yourself.

Don't Be Sexist: Regardless of how pretty or handsome your crush is, don't drop compliments every minute such as, "You are so beautiful!"; "You are so fit. Do you workout?" No matter how well-intentioned you are, you won't be taken seriously if you do this too much. And by all means, don't send nudes.

STARTED IN THE DM

Don't Try Too Hard: Keeping the conversation going should be a two-way street. It is okay to take the initiative to make contact but that doesn't mean try so hard that you come across as thirsty or make the conversation awkward. Don't start bringing up random topics or cracking too many jokes to keep the conversation going. The easiest way to keep the conversation going is by using what is widely referred to as the "F.O.R.D" questions.

- **F-amily:** Ask about their family. For instance, ask about where they grew up, where their family lives, how their siblings are doing, how often they visit, and so on.
- **O-ccupation:** Ask your crush what they do for a living, projects they are working on, their future goals, and the most difficult and fulfilling aspects of their work.
- **R-ecreation:** Ask what they do in their leisure time, how social they are, and what they do for fun.
- **D-reams:** Ask about their biggest dreams and what they would do if they had every resource and could travel anywhere.

Don't "R.A.P.E": At this stage, do not ask questions about R-eligion, A-bortion, P-olitics, and their E-x. Just don't.

Don't Lie: Our lies have a way of catching up to us sooner rather than later. While you can lie to look cool today, remember that you may eventually meet this person and then your lies will be your undoing.

Don't Be Negative: Don't share too many sad stories or discuss pessimistic topics with your online crush so that they can start feeling sorry for you. People don't date those they pity! To keep them interested, focus your conversations on positive topics.

The Do's

Ask Questions After Answering: Remember that it takes two to have a conversation, so don't simply answer questions from the other party and then keep quiet. After answering, do your best to keep the conversation going by asking questions and showing that you are interested, too.

Ask Open-Ended Questions: Refuse to ask yes/no questions or questions that bring one-word answers. (For example: "How was your day?" "Do you go out often?") Instead, ask more open-ended questions that require vivid descriptions. "Tell me about your day? What activities do you do for fun?"

Carry the Conversation at First: It's easy to get angry and kill the conversation once the other person is not asking any questions. However, always try to give people some time by carrying the conversation at first. Show your interest and keep making interesting conversation for as long as you can.

Focus on Similarities: Our similarities bring us together, and this is why we all share traits with our close friends. As you are chatting with your crush, don't gloss over any similarities. If the other person mentions anything similar to you, point out that you've had a similar experience or that you share the same interests.

Ask for Explanations: Another way to improve and keep the conversation going is to also ask for clarification. When your crush mentions anything you are not familiar with, ask them to explain it. Give Compliments: Giving compliments to your crush helps to feed their self-esteem, and they get to feel good about themselves. However, the only way this works is if your compliments are genuine and not exaggerated.

As you can see, it's quite easy to start doing the wrong things when messaging your crush. Luckily, you will be able to avoid the easy traps by keeping what we've shared in mind.

Having a meaningful online conversation can lead your crush to want to take it offline. Therefore, let's make sure you don't completely turn them off in the process.

Chapter 3
Turn Ons & Turn Offs

♥ ♥ ♥ ♥

CHAPTER 3 - TURN-ONS & TURN-OFFS

AS YOU START DATING ONLINE, YOU WILL COME IN CONTACT WITH PEOPLE FROM VARIOUS **BACKGROUNDS, EXPERIENCES, AND BELIEFS**. THIS IS WHY YOU MUST BE AWARE OF THE THINGS YOU SAY AND THE ACTIONS YOU TAKE IN ORDER TO NOT TURN OFF YOUR CRUSH.

The Things You Shouldn't Do

Trying Too Hard to Impress

This applies to both men and women—but especially to men. Don't try too hard to impress your crush by always sending obnoxious jokes and pictures, bragging about your achievements, or telling elaborate and deep stories about your life.

While you should always try to keep a conversation going, don't force it. You don't have to talk about how you stole your dad's car in high school or name-drop celebrities that you met or know. It comes across as lame.

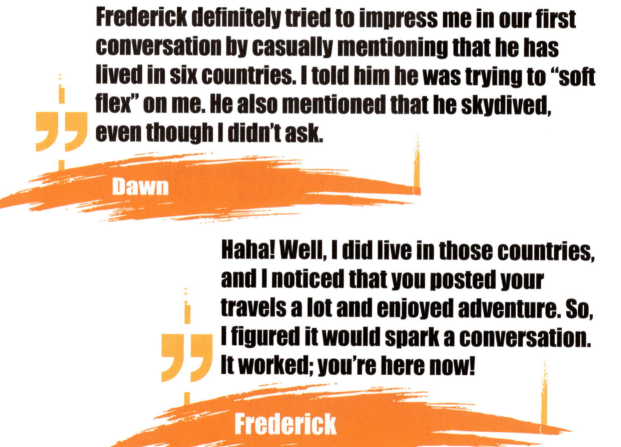

> Frederick definitely tried to impress me in our first conversation by casually mentioning that he has lived in six countries. I told him he was trying to "soft flex" on me. He also mentioned that he skydived, even though I didn't ask.
>
> **Dawn**

> Haha! Well, I did live in those countries, and I noticed that you posted your travels a lot and enjoyed adventure. So, I figured it would spark a conversation. It worked; you're here now!
>
> **Frederick**

CHAPTER 3 - TURN-ONS & TURN-OFFS

Not Accepting No

Fatal flaw #1: You keep messaging a person who is clearly uninterested and stating reasons why you are a perfect match. Please never do this. Don't beg for attention or try to convince someone to be interested in you.

If at any time you ask your crush out and he or she says no, take that no as the end and move on. Online, people don't play hard to get. Even if they do, they'll message you later after you have ignored them for a while. Bottom line, don't chase. The attraction has to be mutual for it to work.

Being Insecure

When you are communicating with your crush, be careful not to mention your insecurities about dating, because it's a big turn-off. Don't mention your hesitations about "this online dating thing" or that you are just trying it out.

No need to say that you have never done this before. Even if you haven't, no one will believe you. Keep the focus on more positive issues, such as the attraction developing between you two and how you are looking forward to meeting him/her.

Taking Too long

Most women want to be pursued and want the man to choose them. As a result, an issue women often complain about is their love interests taking too long to ask for their phone numbers or invite them on a date. Usually, this comes down to a man's fear of being rejected.
(Ladies, avoid asking a man for a date so that the guy does not interpret that as an invitation for sex.)

On the other hand, some men wait for the woman to ask them for their contact information as confirmation that she is interested. Either way, both parties are waiting for the other party to make a move.

43

STARTED IN THE DM

Here's a best practice: Once you realize that you are into a person that you are chatting with, proceed to ask them to take the communication offline with the intention of going on a date.

It's that simple.

It makes no sense to wait. The rule is that once you are chatting for a few days, take it offline. Not doing this will only turn your crush off, and they will stop returning your messages.

Frederick asked for my phone number in our first conversation. I was enjoying our chat, and I was interested in getting to know him better. But I also did not want him to take my number and text me to death or hit me with constant "WYD" messages. I told him he could have my number but that he had to "use it for what it's for".

Dawn

I knew when she said "use it for what it's for" that she meant she wanted me to call her and not text. That made her stand out above other women I had talked to in the past. She definitely set her communication expectations upfront. I called her the next day, and we spoke for three hours on our first call.

Frederick

CHAPTER 3 - TURN-ONS & TURN-OFFS

Making Requests

Since their inception, all dating sites have been known to contain charlatans, weirdos, and fraudsters. Many dating platforms have now adopted complex algorithms to help weed out these accounts; yet some still slip through the cracks. We all know how many fake and impersonation accounts exist on Instagram so you never really know who you are talking to until you can put a face to a name.

The last thing you want to do is send signals to your crush and to the algorithms that you are a fraudster. Ironically, this is what a lot of newbies do. They end up making demands that get them reported, blacklisted, and then banned.

This should go without saying, but please do not make demands from your crush. No matter how fast you hit it off or how close you become, don't ask them for anything. Don't ask your crush for any nudes, gift cards, money, or gifts of any kind.

Expecting Too Much Too Soon

Remember that your crush owes you nothing. So, don't get angry if they don't come online when you are online or if they don't return your calls. Don't start acting jealous or start making unnecessary demands

STARTED IN THE DM

such as asking them not to chat with other people, monitoring their likes and comments, or expecting them to constantly occupy their time online chatting with you.

This is the fastest way to turn your crush off.

Do More of These Instead

Be Seen as Responsible

One of the most off-putting habits in online dating is not replying or following up with your dates. Unfortunately, entrepreneurs are particularly notorious for doing this because of our busy schedules. This is where you have to be careful about the promises you make to your online crush. Don't promise to come online when you know you wouldn't be able to. Don't ignore their messages for days and then give excuses. If you are not ready to be serious with online dating, you shouldn't bother about it until you are ready to dedicate some time to it. This is because being seen as irresponsible or not being able to keep your word is a huge turn-off for most people. It's important to keep to your promises online and offline.

Have a Plan

You are more likely to get dates when you have clear plans. People generally don't want to go out with someone with vague ideas. Having a plan instantly elevates you above the multitude of suitors out there. It communicates that you are thoughtful and intentional, and it makes it easier for your crush to say yes since you've saved them the stress of planning.

Be Honest

It's tempting to lie in your profile and chat conversations to look cool and

CHAPTER 3 - TURN-ONS & TURN-OFFS

impressive. However, as I stated before, the issue with lying is that it will eventually turn on you. You don't know how knowledgeable your crush is going to be about a particular topic you lied about. You also never know who knows who. The world is most likely too small to keep your lie around forever, so sooner or later your cover will be blown.

Now, being honest is not an excuse to start advertising your inadequacies to everyone you meet.

Simply be honest about who you are and your capabilities, and don't misrepresent yourself. If you plan to meet your crush offline, your online lies will crumble—so keep it real.

Chapter 4
Moving Offline
♥ ♥ ♥ ♥

STARTED IN THE DM

THE PROBLEM WITH ONLINE DATING IS THAT MOST PEOPLE DON'T UNDERSTAND THAT ONLINE DATING IS NOT ACTUALLY "DATING".

Online is just a tool that can lead to dating in real life. It's like the date before the "real date". This means that everything you do online should be geared toward having an amazing dating life in real life.

Most likely, your goal in online dating is to either find a fun and short-term relationship or serious and long-term one. You can't successfully achieve either of these goals with a virtual partner. It's

CHAPTER 4 - MOVING OFFLINE

neither productive nor reasonable to try to make your crush fall in love with you online if your goal is to have a *real* relationship. The only way to do this is to take it offline and confirm the connection is real.

Have a Friendly Conversation

Once you can get a conversation going with your crush, your job at that moment is to keep it up. It is not the time to start testing some psychological tricks on your crush.

Instead, try your best to keep the conversation open on the path to getting to know each other on a deeper level. Ask them about their jobs, hobbies, dreams, and likes. You can use the F.O.R.D technique discussed in Chapter 2. During this stage, remember to also still respect their boundaries. Don't start telling them you love them and all, because it's not possible. You can tell them you like their pictures, but don't start being ridiculous.

Your aim at this stage is to move from being a complete stranger to being an acquaintance—not to all of a sudden be in an immediate relationship.

Talk More Than Text

Moving from chatting on social and dating platforms to talking on the phone (without first meeting in person) can be awkward for some. The good news is that most dating platforms now offer a lifesaver: video calls. These days, quality video calls are now readily available on many platforms for free. Even if your dating platform doesn't offer it, you can easily do a video call by migrating to FaceTime, Facebook Messenger, Instagram video call, and so on.

51

STARTED IN THE DM

There is no reason to be catfished in the 21st century.

Video calls are the perfect middle ground between online chatting and meeting in real life. The thought of this makes many people nervous, but you should know that the benefits of making calls far outweigh the inconveniences. Online chemistry is different from real-life chemistry. Observing someone's mannerisms, hearing their voice and how they speak, and feeling their energy can either be a huge turnoff or a beautiful turn-on.

Make that video call as soon as possible!

So, after chatting for a few hours or even a couple of days, proceed to ask for a quick video call. There are ways you can make this sound non-threatening. One way is to tell them that you just want to see their face and connect. If the feeling is mutual, they will not object. There is no denying the need for face-to-face interaction when building a relationship, even if it is virtual.

As time goes on, you get used to seeing each other's faces and hearing each other's voices. This will reduce the surprise and awkwardness when you see each other for the first time in real life.

That said, it's surprising that most people are unaware of how helpful video calls can be. Having a video call helps to solve many major common problems associated with online dating, which are:

- Scams
- False signals
- Fake/impersonator accounts

One, you get to identify scammers because they will never agree to a video call with you. They'll keep making obnoxious demands, such as saying they are out of the country or need your bank details to process funds.

The other benefit is identifying false signals. A lot of people upload old

52

CHAPTER 4 - MOVING OFFLINE

pictures that don't accurately communicate their current looks. On the other hand, some people are far more beautiful and interesting than their profiles make them to be.

In these instances, their profile sends false signals, and unless you do a video call, you might not even be that interested in them.

> I remember the first time we talked on FaceTime; I was looking in the background to see what his house looked like and if he was clean. My pet peeve is a messy house, lol. I was happy with what I saw though. I was like, "Yeah, he's fine."

Dawn

> What?! I didn't know you were looking at my house, but I should have figured. I was happy to see that she looked like she did on Instagram—even better!

Frederick

STARTED IN THE DM

Ask Your Crush Out

As we've been saying, online dating is not really dating; it's a tool. To make use of that tool, the end goal is to ask your crush out.

It makes no sense to wait too long before asking your crush out. After a few conversations and video dates, you will know if you want to meet in person or not. Go ahead and take the next step to invite your crush on a date. If you don't ask him/her on a date, they could assume that you are not really interested or that you are wasting their time.

You can easily schedule a meetup by saying, "Hey, it's been lovely talking with you so far. I would love a meet-up." That said, it's important that you frame your sentence as a concrete desire and not as an insecure wish. We're emphasizing this because many people ask out their crush the wrong way.

The wrong way to ask your crush out is saying, "Hey, I've enjoyed our conversations so far. Wanna meet up?" While some people won't have any problem with this, it's not decisive enough, and it will cause many to turn you down. You don't want to ask your crush if he or she wants to go out with you. Instead, you want to tell them you want to take them out.

You are more likely to get a positive response when you ask directly. Once you have chatted for a while, tell them you are ready for the next step, which is meeting them in the real world.

Also, be careful not to push your crush too much when asking for a date. Don't force them to commit to a weekend. Instead, go easy by asking them out on a weeknight or a quick meetup on the weekend. By doing this, you reduce the burden associated with an elaborate date.

54

CHAPTER 4 - MOVING OFFLINE

> We lived in different cities so going on our first date took planning. She flew to the city I lived in, and we made plans. She said that she was coming for business, but I knew she was really coming to see me.

Frederick

> I was actually the one who initiated meeting up in person. We had been talking on the phone and on video for a month, and I suggested that I fly to the city he lived in. I could handle some business while there, and we could go on a date. I paid for my own flight and booked my hotel. I did not expect him to pay for my travel because I did not want him to have any expectations of me.

Dawn

Chapter 5
How to Have a Great Date

NOW WE ARE AT THE MOST FUN AND INTERESTING STAGE OF ONLINE DATING: THE REAL-LIFE MEETING

Most people assume that dates are easy, and they can just go out to meet a stranger and connect with no problem. This is a false assumption that leads to tons of failed dates. The ideas most people have about having a real date are not realistic, and that's why we are focusing on how to plan and execute a great date in this chapter. We'll start with the most commonly selected dating locations.

Where Should You Go?

What most people do is invite their date to a restaurant or a bar nearby. This is the conventional go-to plan, and it's what we see in the movies. However, there's a major flaw in this dating approach.

It's boring.

STARTED IN THE DM

The drawback of conventional date locations such as dark bars, pubs, and late-night restaurants is that they offer you nothing to do apart from talking. There is nothing interesting to do or comment on. In most cases, someone ends up on their phone (which is a dating no-no by the way).

The widespread addiction to gadgets has made us all good at online conversation, while it has simultaneously weakened our real-life communication skills.

Betting that you'll be able to find the spark in a dark restaurant over a 3-hour meal is not reasonable. Unless you are a great conversationalist, you are better off having a date at an unconventional location rather than staring at each other for hours.

The key to a great date is taking your date to a fun and entertaining setting like amusement parks, museums, art galleries, bookstores, parks for physical activities, concerts, and more.

You may be thinking, "What if my crush isn't interested in all this?" Our answer is that you don't have to take all your online dates to the same locations. Finding great locations is as easy as going through your date's profiles or asking about their hobbies before asking them out. For example, if he or she is into arts, you can visit an exhibit. If they are into bowling, you can go bowling.

But it doesn't have to be about them entirely; it can be about you, too. You can take your crush to the locations you usually feel at home in hopes that they'll love it as well.

To get the location right, we've listed a few suggestions. An ideal setting is usually a location where you can:
- Move around easily.
- See interesting things.
- Participate in activities.
- Talk freely.

60

CHAPTER 5 - HOW TO HAVE A GREAT DATE

Possible venues include museums, playgrounds, music festivals, fairs, game floors, art exhibitions, tourist attraction centers, movie theaters, and so on.

The beauty of these locations is that no matter how your dating partner behaves, you can still have a good time doing something fun.

The bottom line is that it's much better to take your crush to locations where you have other things to do apart from talking. Mind you, talking is good. But unfortunately, it's simply not good enough to make your dates memorable. Unconventional locations help to diffuse the tension and awkwardness and both of you will be able to act like your natural selves.

Fun Fact:
If you are reluctant to commit to a date and only eager to meet your crush, you can ask your date to join you for simple activities such as grabbing a bite to eat at a local coffee shop, working out together, or taking a walk down the street.

STARTED IN THE DM

This saves time and helps you to decide whether to cut things short if you don't see the relationship going anywhere or to set up a proper date later on.

Digging Deeper

If you take a good look around, you'll realize that you have a great deal of things in common with your friends. Chances are you and your friends visit the same places, work at the same place, have similar habits, read the same type of books, and so on.

As humans, our similarities bring us together, and our differences split us apart! Therefore, for a connection to be created between you and your crush, you should both share about yourselves and bring your similarities to the forefront. It's time to dig deeper to see if this person is a possible love connection or if they will forever live in the 'friend zone'.

Determining if a person is partner material takes time, but you can speed up the process by asking intentional questions and discussing a variety of subjects to gauge your alignment. Some great topics to cover include:

- Spirituality
- Family Goals
- Life Goals
- Finances
- Career and Lifestyle
- Habits and Interests
- Purpose

CHAPTER 5 -   HOW TO HAVE A GREAT DATE

As you disclose personal information on these various topics, your similarities will come to the surface, and from there, you are likely to grow closer.

While we don't advise asking your dates a list of canned questions, according to a psychological study by Dr. Arthur Aron, it's been proven that certain questions actually help strangers connect quickly. Here are some of the questions:

- If you were able to live to the age of 90 and retain either the mind or body of a 30-year-old for the last 60 years of your life, which would you choose?
- Name three things you and your partner appear to have in common.
- For what in your life do you feel most grateful?
- If you could change anything about the way you were raised, what would it be?
- If you could wake up tomorrow having gained one quality or ability, what would it be?
- Given the choice of anyone in the world, who would you want as a dinner guest?
- What would constitute a perfect day for you?
- Is there something that you've dreamt of doing for a long time? Why haven't you done it?
- What is the greatest accomplishment of your life?
- What do you value most in a friendship?
- What is your most treasured memory, and what is your most terrible memory?
- What roles do love and affection play in your life?
- Your house, containing everything you own, catches fire. After saving your loved ones and pets, you have time to safely make a final dash to save any one item. What would it be? Why?

If you were going to become a close friend with your partner, please share what would be important for him or her to know.

63

Share a personal problem and ask your partner's advice on how he or she might handle it. Also, ask your partner to reflect to you how you seem to be feeling about the problem you have chosen.

By asking these and similar personal questions, you get to know each other better. You'll both realize how compatible you are and whether you're both ready to take the plunge of seeing each other regularly.

Communicate Your Intentions

Make your feelings and intentions known to your crush on the date. If you are really into them, let them know. If you find their looks amazing or their intellect dazzling, let them know.

If you are interested in taking things further, let them know. Equally, if you are also not into them, let them know politely that you are not ready to date right now. Do not waste a person's time or lead them on.

Be Conscious of Time

When you take your crush out on a date, be conscious of the time you spend with them. Don't be too rigid about spending hours with them. Make sure you are considerate of their time and ask if they have to leave at a certain hour.

Quality time is quality time. A date can be as short as 30 minutes or as long as 6 hours.

You have to realize that the best thing about a date is the experience and

CHAPTER 5 - HOW TO HAVE A GREAT DATE

not the duration.

If at any time you see that your date is getting bored or tired, kindly end the date and schedule the next one. No matter how smitten you are, don't prolong the date just to spend more time with your crush. This could backfire on you.

> **We really hit it off on our first date. We ended up making it a 3-day straight date. The vibe was right. I felt like he really understood me.**
>
> **Dawn**

> **I knew we would get along well because when I picked her up from the airport it was in the morning and we are both busy entrepreneurs who work. She was cool with us going to a WeWork and working together for a few hours before going on our lunch date. I appreciated that she understood my lifestyle as an entrepreneur, and she didn't trip when I had to take a call or check my phone during the day.**
>
> **Frederick**

65

STARTED IN THE DM

How To Maintain Progress

Having a great first date doesn't mean you are out of the woods yet; things can still go wrong if you don't follow up. Our recommendation is to always set up the second date on the first date because most people don't like uncertainty. The best way to communicate that you enjoyed meeting them is to plan the next meeting before you depart. Even if your first date ends in a bedroom, don't disappear the following morning. Wait and communicate that you are interested in them for real.

Tell them that you will love to meet them again and tell them when. Inform them of possible locations, and don't leave until you've planned out the second date. If your date is into you, he or she will agree to the second date, and with that, you've maintained progress.

People are not mind readers, and everyone is not emotionally intelligent and able to read social cues. If you are not interested in another date, let them know—being direct and honest is always the best path.

Move at The Pace That Works for You

Now that you know the interest is mutual, continue to build the relationship. Meeting in person can create a spark, and things could become physical or affectionate. However, it is important to maintain the foundation of the relationship—conversation.

Studies from the University of Finland revealed that having some time elapse between dates helps to strengthen the relationship, and we agree. We lived in different states at the beginning of our relationship, so since we were not able to spend time in person, we were forced to communicate. In hindsight, we believe it makes our relationship stronger because we really got to know each other before things became physical.

CHAPTER 5 - *HOW TO HAVE A GREAT DATE*

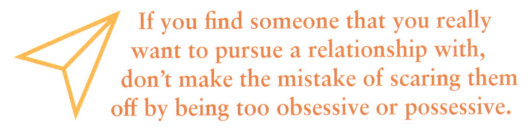

If you find someone that you really want to pursue a relationship with, don't make the mistake of scaring them off by being too obsessive or possessive.

Take things slowly, or at least at a mutual pace. Having a great first date is not an excuse to start seeing and talking every day — unless that is what you both want. In our case, we spoke every single day after our first conversation on the phone. It was not an expectation, it just flowed naturally. Just because a person does not call or text you every day it doesn't mean they are not interested; it is important to learn your potential partner's communication style.

Some people don't like to text; some don't like to talk on the phone a lot. Some people work random hours. Don't leave things up to assumptions—simply ask them how often they want to communicate. Some people will advise you to slow down and ease yourself into the relationship, give space between the dates, and give the relationship time to mature. We think you should do what feels right for you.

> **We were only talking for two months before he asked me to make it official. We talked on the phone every day for two months, spent three days together, and we both knew we had something special between us. I loved that he went for what he wanted and let me know he was serious about me. It was very different from men that I dated in the past, who were indecisive or played games.**
>
> **Dawn**

> **I knew pretty fast that she was someone I could see myself with. I had to go ahead and make it official before someone else did. I recognized she had the qualities I was looking for, so why continue to look any further?**
>
> **Frederick**

67

Chapter 6
Moving Up the Ladder

STARTED IN THE DM

AT THE END OF THE DAY, DATING IS STILL A NUMBERS GAME, AND THE MORE DATES YOU GO ON, THE BETTER OFF YOU ARE.

That said, it's a game that you get better at as time goes on. As you go on dates repeatedly, you'll be able to constantly work on yourself, improve your conversations and hone your seduction skills. However, because it's a numbers game, realize that not every date will progress into a relationship. We've gone on several dates only to realize our dates were people we didn't want to start a relationship with.

Some dates will fail to go beyond the first or second one. This could be due to a lack of interest from you, your date, or the both of you. It's also common to have things fizzle out after the second or third date when you realize your partner is not someone you want to be with.

On the other hand, there are times when everything seems to click. You and your partner will get off to a great start, and things will get better as time goes on. Now, once this happens, it's time to move up the ladder toward a proper relationship.

70

CHAPTER 6 - MOVING UP THE LADDER

STARTED IN THE DM

Start Seeing Each Other Regularly

Many couples started seeing each other regularly right from the first date, and they are doing fine today. On the other hand, many couples found success waiting till the second or third date to accelerate the relationship. Then, there are those people who wait months, or years, to decide what they want—stay away from that kind of thing.

What we recommend you look for before you start an intimate relationship is signs of reciprocity. No matter how shy or eccentric your date is, you should be sure that they have an interest in you before you kick off a relationship.

You shouldn't be the only one doing the calling, chatting, and date planning.

When you don't contact them for a day or two, expect them to miss you and ask about you. You should watch out for this reciprocity before committing to someone.

You don't want to have a pseudo-relationship with someone who is not interested in you. However, once you see enough signs that your partner is trying, you can commit to seeing them regularly.

Respect Boundaries

The topic of boundaries doesn't get the attention it deserves. To save yourself a number of headaches, try your best to respect your partner's boundaries once you are in a relationship. While some people are okay with elegant displays of affection, such as weekly date nights, everyday

CHAPTER 6 - MOVING UP THE LADDER

texting, and so on. Other people like a simpler relationship.

Knowing what to do in these instances will depend on your communication skills. We all come from different cultures, and we have different experiences; therefore, we can't all like the same things. Everyone has their particular likes and dislikes regarding their intimate relationships.

To move from dating to being lovers, you need to learn what your partner likes and dislikes and communicate yours too. Not only should you be aware of these things but also respect them.

Communication is key. If you don't learn to communicate and respect each other's boundaries, you will continue to cross those boundaries and eventually ruin the relationship.

Travel & Go on Adventures Together

Once you are seeing each other regularly, it's easy to relax on the exciting things you did to win your partner's heart while dating and slow everything down to a crawl.

Please don't do this. Keep things exciting and fresh.

Even if you can no longer go out every third weeknight and weekend, make plans and keep going on various adventures together. Instead of toning things down, your best option is to raise the tempo.

As the weeks go by, make big plans with your partner and travel together. Go on a road trip, climb a mountain together if you are into that sort of thing, or go camping. The major benefit of doing this is that it relaxes the tension and allows the both of you to be your real selves. When everything slows down, it's easier to pretend to be the perfect boyfriend or girlfriend. But, when you are out there taking adventures

73

often, you get to see your partner when stressed, angry, and happy. You get to fall in and out of love over and over again and see if there's a possible future to the relationship.

Meet Friends & Family

There comes a time in every relationship when you have to meet your partner's friends and family.

We recommend that unless you are ready for a long-term relationship, you should avoid meeting the family of your partner. When you can't avoid meeting them (e.g., your partner lives with their parents or he/she lives with kids), try your best to restrict your conversation with the family to neutral topics. You don't want to be seen by the parents as the fiancée who dumped their daughter or by the kids as the playboy boyfriend who dumped their mom. Be mindful.

Keep Your Relationship Private

The penultimate point we'll be discussing is the golden rule of all lasting relationships: **maintain privacy at all costs.**

Having a beautiful and long-term relationship is not easy. But one tip that helps is to keep your personal business private. You should always try to keep the matters of your relationship private and this has to do with the boundaries we mentioned earlier. You should communicate with your partner that you would like two things:
1. No interference from friends and family
2. Not having an active social media presence for the relationship and keeping it offline.

CHAPTER 6 - MOVING UP THE LADDER

Too much interference from outsiders tends to suffocate those in the relationship. Both partners won't be able to act like themselves since there are unrealistic expectations for them. This also leads to a buildup of resentment over time, and this is exactly why you shouldn't have friends and family interfering in your personal business.

Once there's a quarrel or misunderstanding, you should both act like adults and unite to find solutions and not communicate it with everyone. Every misstep in the relationship shouldn't become public knowledge. Also, having a constant social media presence for your relationship adds unnecessary strain. People start keeping tabs on your posts, and once you stop posting each other, you may start getting calls and comments from people asking for an explanation. Don't open that door.

Keeping the relationship online can also lead to unnecessary fights when a partner fails to upload the right picture or does not comment on or like a picture uploaded by the partner. There's also the risk of a partner sharing sensitive information about the relationship online that ends up breaking the intimacy.

There's simply a lot that can go wrong so it's better to keep everything offline. The best thing is to keep to a private relationship in which you can be free to act and breathe without any external interference or expectations.

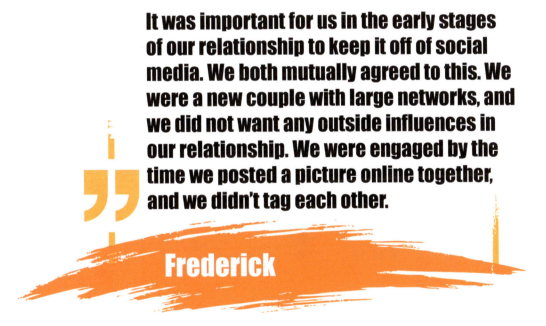

> It was important for us in the early stages of our relationship to keep it off of social media. We both mutually agreed to this. We were a new couple with large networks, and we did not want any outside influences in our relationship. We were engaged by the time we posted a picture online together, and we didn't tag each other.
>
> Frederick

STARTED IN THE DM

> It was important for us to have a solid foundation before sharing our relationship with the world. We met online in October, met in person in November, became a couple in December, got engaged in February, and married in March. I remember the first time I posted that I was married, people were shocked; they asked, "to who?" From their perspective, he seemed to come out of nowhere.
>
> **Dawn**

Relationship Work - Life Balance

We'll be ending this book with ideas that will help you balance your relationship with your work-life as an entrepreneur. We've been through this, and we know it can be very difficult. The good news is that we've successfully balanced our love with our work, and you can too!
As long as you are dedicated, you can successfully balance your work-life by following these ideas:

Face it head-on

The mistake most couples make is that they don't talk about maintaining the balance. This is a big mistake. You have to shed as much light as possible on this for it to work. Don't just flow ahead with the relationship. Hash out your beliefs and needs around boundaries, affection, finances, and so on. Make rules, which may cover when to come home, when to have some personal time without phone interruptions, how to split the bills, and so on.

Talk about finances first

We've discovered that a lot of arguments surround money, so this is

CHAPTER 6 - MOVING UP THE LADDER

where you want to start. You need to have difficult conversations early on, such as how to manage your financial goals and savings. Talk about how to support each other if a job is lost and how to allocate money for home and work. Talk about relocation and how future goals will affect the time of your partner.

Be unconditionally supportive

Unconditional forgiveness and understanding are two crucial ingredients to every successful relationship. It's important to realize that you might have to make sacrifices and show concern for your spouse even if you're extremely tired. Don't start a fight anytime your partner spends more time on their work; instead, be supportive. We make it a priority to show support for each other, and it's one of the reasons why our relationship is so balanced.

Share household duties

As simple as household chores seem, it's often a reason for escalated arguments among couples. To avoid this, set strict roles for who takes out the trash, who does the dishes, who cooks, who vacuums, and so on. Make the roles balanced to fit each other's schedule. Also, don't be afraid to seek help and look for alternatives. For example, you can hire house cleaning services and cook your meals in bulk and then refrigerate them.

Balance sacrifices

If one of you wants to pursue a large career goal, the other will inevitably need to make some sacrifices. It's important to respect these sacrifices and pay them back. Balance is important for the long term. So, communicate with your partner that if one of you makes a sacrifice, they have to be repaid, as a partner can keep making sacrifices for the other while the other does nothing.

Apologize and forgive

There's no perfect relationship, and relationships can be the headquarters of stress and hurt feelings. However, holding grudges or being stubborn helps no one. Always prioritize communication and be ready to apologize and forgive for the sake of the relationship.
In March 2021, after our first anniversary, we decided to write this book to tell our story and encourage other single professionals to consider online dating as a viable option to find a partner.

We always laugh when we tell our story about finding love "in the DM", and we are always pleasantly surprised to hear the stories from other couples who share this experience. There are no rules to dating and marriage; it is important to do

CHAPTER 6 - MOVING UP THE LADDER

what is best aligned with you.

What has helped us to keep our relationship healthy?

- Putting our relationship first
- Never going to other people to talk about our challenges or issues with each other
- Being committed to resolving conflict in a healthy way
- Taking the other person's feelings into account
- Seeking help from our life coach and marriage counselor (The premarital sessions were especially helpful for us.)
- Doing regular check-ins with each other to talk about how we are doing as a wife/husband and discussing ways that we can improve on a personal level.
- We are both very self aware and realize that we are new to this. We understand that we have to approach marriage as we would anything else where we are a novice—this means with an open mind and a willingness to always learn.
- We would like to close by thanking our family and friends for their support, non-judgment, and for welcoming us with open arms on both sides. It has been truly beautiful to watch our families and networks merge. The overwhelming love and support from those we love have helped to keep our bond strong.

#startedinthedm

Do you have a story about finding love online? Share it with us at startedintheDM@gmail.com and on our Instagram @StartedIntheDM.

Tag us for an opportunity to be featured.

About the Authors

@dawnwdickson

Dawn Dickson-Akpoghene is a serial entrepreneur and inventor with over 20 years of experience in technology, marketing and business development. She has founded five successful cash flow positive companies since 2001, including Flat Out of Heels (2011) and PopCom (2017) and is considered to be a pioneer in the equity crowdfunding space.

Dawn has received numerous awards and accolades including being recognized on the inaugural Forbes Next 1000 List, listed among INC Magazine's 100 top Female Founders, and being named the 2020 OBWS Black Entrepreneur of the Year presented by Snapchat. Dawn has been featured in countless media outlets including the cover of Black Enterprise magazine, Fortune, Fast Company, Venture Beat, Huff Post, Essence Magazine, and more. Dawn has an expertise in raising traditional and non-traditional business capital, having raised millions of dollars for her ventures since 2001. In 2019, Dawn became the first female founder globally to raise a secure token offering (STO) of over $1M using equity crowdfunding; her total as of 2021 exceeds $5M from over 7000 investors globally.

Dawn is a seasoned professional speaker, business coach, author, advisor and angel investor. She currently resides between Miami, FL, and Columbus, OH, with her husband Frederick and daughter, Nia.

@abovav_mind

Kevbe Frederick Akpoghene is a 4X founder, celebrity technologist, software engineer, and entertainment businessman. His software development company Abovav, is a trusted technology partner to hundreds of businesses and start-ups around the world. He is the mastermind behind four multimillion-dollar companies, namely Abovav Technologies, Scizzrs Inc., JéGo Technologies Inc., and Oddio Entertainment.

Leveraging his robust experience in software engineering and business, Frederick founded JéGo, a technology company focused on building a new logistics network to support local community businesses. JéGo Pods brings the personal care services (such as COVID testing, IV drips) and products you need to your location with the power of autonomous, driverless technology. His other company, Scizzrs, has also witnessed tremendous growth and has been listed as one of the Top 11 Companies to Invest in for 2020 & 2021. He also became a NASDAQ Milestone Maker (Fall 2020).

Oddio Entertainment, LLC, which he invested in and built together with his brother, Tejiri, has produced and written for the music industry's big names such as Major Lazer, Tems, Beenie Man, Tolani, and many others. The son of a celebrity artist /architect, Frederick Akpoghene is very passionate about art and spends his free time collecting fine arts from various places. Frederick is also a seasoned growth hacker, A&R, author, advisor, and angel investor. He currently resides between Miami, FL, and Columbus, OH, with his wife Dawn, and daughter, Nia.

@startedinthedm

startedinthedm.com

CPSIA information can be obtained
at www.ICGtesting.com
Printed in the USA
LVHW070453310122
709808LV00002B/17